We are truly honored that you've chosen our apartment for your stay and as a token of our gratitude, we are delighted to present you with this book. It delves into a subject that holds a special place in our hearts, one that we find endlessly fascinating and enriching. This book represents more than just our interests—it's a gesture of our appreciation for your decision to stay with us and a hope that you may find the topic as captivating as we do. May this gift not only serve as a memento of your time here but also spark curiosity, inspire new thoughts, and perhaps even ignite a passion similar to ours. Thank you for being our guests, and we sincerely hope you enjoy this book and your stay in our beloved apartment.

Yours sincerely,

Pablo

Investment in land

Grow your real estate assets from scratch

Content

Prologue: This is not a prologue

This is not a prologue, it is a LEAP. You will understand later.

Let me tell you the story of Juan, a young man who, until the age of 33, had followed the path that his parents had laid out for him. He studied a career that he was not passionate about, got a **stable** job in a company where he did not feel fulfilled and lived a life that did not make him happy.

One day, after much reflection and conversations with friends and family, he realised that he was living the life his parents wanted for him and not the life he wanted for himself. He decided to take charge of his life and discover what his true passion was. After a long process of introspection, Juan discovered that his true passion was working in the world of fashion, an industry he had always been interested in but had put aside for fear of letting his family down.

Juan realised that he had wasted many years doing what others expected of him and had not invested time in learning and developing his true passion. So he began to study and work in the fashion world, first as a volunteer and then as an employee of a local shop. Eventually, Juan started to develop his career in the fashion world and managed to have his own company. He discovered that success is not only measured by money, but by the satisfaction of doing what you love and living the life you want.

John's story reminds us that sometimes we can live the life that others expect of us rather than the life we really want. It is important that we ask ourselves hard questions and be honest with ourselves about what really makes us happy.

Sometimes it can be difficult to know where to start in the pursuit of our true passion and how to achieve our financial goals. This book is designed to help you set clear goals, plan for your financial future, and discover how to invest in real estate for a fuller, more satisfying life. I will teach you how to identify real estate investment opportunities and evaluate properties to determine if they are right for you.

However, this book is more than just an investment guide. It is a call to action to change your approach to life. Many times, we get stuck in our comfort zone and refuse to learn and improve. But, if you want to succeed in any area of life, you need to be willing to learn and change.

This book is just the beginning of your journey to a healthier financial life. I encourage you to take the lessons written here and apply them to your daily life. Continue to learn and grow in your knowledge of real estate investing and personal finance.

Remember, financial education is not just for those who want to get rich. It is for everyone who wants to take control of their finances and live a healthy and prosperous financial life.

I hope this book will help you find that passion and give you the tools you need to achieve a healthier financial life. Remember, it's never too late to learn and make positive changes in your life.

So, without further ado, I invite you to dive into the pages of this book and you may end up finding the real estate frog that hides within its pages.

I. Introduction to real estate investment

I.I Why is financial education and investment in real estate important? Who should read this book and what can they expect from it?

Financial education and real estate investing are two closely related concepts. Financial education is essential for anyone who wants to be successful in any type of investment, and investing in real estate is one of the best ways to invest and increase wealth in the long term.

First, financial education is important because it gives you the tools and knowledge you need to make smart financial decisions and grow your money. This includes learning basic concepts such as budgeting and credit management, as well as knowledge of more advanced investments such as the stock market and the real estate market.

Financial education is a topic that has become increasingly important in recent years. Throughout history, a lack of financial literacy has led many people to make poor financial decisions, which have had a negative impact on their lives. For example, in the Great Depression of the 1930s, many people lost their savings because they had not diversified their investments and had invested all their money in the stock market. This event had a lasting effect on people's financial awareness, and many began to understand the importance of having a sound financial education.

Since then, financial education has evolved greatly, and there is now a wealth of information and resources available to help people understand and manage their finances more effectively. Despite this, there are still many people who do not have a solid understanding of basic financial concepts, such as saving, investing and budgeting. This can lead to costly financial decisions and can put long-term financial security at risk.

Today, financial education has become a necessity for most people. Whether you are an employee, an entrepreneur or an investor, having a solid understanding of financial concepts is essential to succeed in any field. Moreover, with the increasing complexity of the financial world and the plethora of investment options available, it is more important than ever to have a solid financial education to avoid unnecessary risks and make sound decisions.

Real estate investment is important because it can provide long-term passive income and increase your net worth. Real estate has the potential to increase in value over time, which means you can make a significant profit if you decide to sell it in the future.

The real estate market has been one of the oldest forms of investment and has been one of the main sources of wealth throughout history. Since the first houses were built in the Stone Age, land ownership has been a sign of wealth and power.

In ancient Greece, ownership of land and houses was a measure of personal wealth and was considered a safe and secure investment. In ancient Rome, real estate ownership became a lucrative business, with many investors acquiring large tracts of land to grow crops and sell agricultural products.

Even in the Middle Ages, kings and nobles acquired large tracts of land to increase their wealth and political power. In the 19th century, increased industrialisation and urbanisation created new opportunities for real estate investment. The construction of railways and roads allowed people to move to new areas, creating a demand for housing and commercial premises.

Today, real estate remains a popular and profitable investment. Over the last decade, the value of real estate has increased significantly in many parts of the world. According to the World Bank's annual report, real estate accounts for 60% of global asset value and remains one of the safest and most profitable long-term investments.

An interesting anecdote is that the oldest building still in use as a dwelling is the wooden Horyu-ji house in Nara, Japan, which was built in 710 and is still inhabited. This house is an example of how real estate can be a lasting investment and a source of wealth over the centuries.

Throughout history, real estate investing has been a popular and profitable way to invest. In this book, you will learn how to invest in real estate and how to maximise your financial potential in this exciting industry.

In addition, investing in the real estate market can provide a monthly income stream through property rental. This income can be a reliable and stable source of income over the long term, which means that it can be a good option for those seeking additional passive income.

In terms of who should read this book and what they can expect from it, this book is for anyone interested in learning about investing in the real estate market and how to take advantage of this investment opportunity to increase their wealth over the long term. If you are new to the world of real estate investing, this book will provide you with a solid foundation of knowledge to get you started.

In this book, you will learn about the fundamentals of real estate investing, how to evaluate properties, how to finance a real estate investment, and how to manage a property. We will also discuss topics such as the current real estate market, common challenges facing real estate investors, and strategies for maximising your return on investment.

In short, financial education and real estate investing are critical for those seeking to increase their wealth and secure their financial future. This book is a useful tool for those who wish to learn more about real estate investing and how to take advantage of this opportunity to achieve their long-term financial goals.

I.II What is real estate investment?

Real estate investment is the purchase of real estate with the objective of generating income through rental, resale or development of the property. This is a popular and attractive form of investment for many people because of its potential to generate passive income and increase wealth over the long term.

Successful property investment starts with good planning and a sound investment strategy. Before buying a property, it is important to have a clear understanding of the factors that influence the value of a property and how they can be used to generate income and increase value over time.

There are several factors that can affect the value of a property, such as its location, physical condition, market demand and interest rates. When evaluating a property, it is important to consider these factors and determine whether the property has the potential to generate long-term income.

A very important one is macroeconomics, which refers to the study of the economy as a whole, has a great influence on the real estate sector. Macroeconomic factors, such as inflation, interest rates, economic growth, unemployment and monetary policy, can directly affect the demand and supply of real estate.

For example, during a period of economic growth, demand for real estate tends to increase, as people have more income and are willing to invest in real estate. On the other hand, during an economic downturn, the demand for real estate may decrease, as people have less income and prioritise other needs.

In addition, interest rates can also affect the demand for real estate, as people are less likely to invest in real estate when interest rates are high. On the other hand, low interest rates can stimulate demand for real estate, as people can obtain financing at a lower cost.

In conclusion, macroeconomics is a critical factor affecting the real estate sector. It is important for real estate investors to be aware of macroeconomic changes in order to make informed decisions and take advantage of investment opportunities in the real estate market.

In addition, it is important to understand the different types of property investment available. Common options include buying rental properties, buying and selling properties (known as flipping) and investing in commercial properties. Each type of property investment has different considerations and requirements, so it is important to understand which best suits your goals and financial situation.

Another important factor in real estate investment is property management. Proper management of a property can increase its value and generate steady income. This may involve careful selection of tenants, regular maintenance and repairs, and management of the property's finances.

In summary, property investment can be an effective strategy for generating income and increasing wealth over the long term. However, it is important to have a clear understanding of the factors that influence the value of a property, the investment options available and effective property management to achieve success. In the following chapters, we will delve into each of these topics and more to help you achieve successful property investment.

I.III Reasons for investing in real estate

Real estate investment is one of the most popular and effective ways to invest and grow your money. There are many reasons why investing in real estate is an attractive option for investors, from the potential for long-term returns to the stability and security that real estate offers. In this chapter, we will explore some of the most compelling reasons to invest in real estate.

Long-term earnings potential

One of the main reasons for investing in real estate is the potential for long-term returns. Unlike other forms of investment, such as the stock market, real estate has the potential to increase in value over time. If you buy a property in a good location and hold it for an extended period of time, you are likely to see a significant increase in value. In addition, you can earn a steady income stream through renting out the property, which can further increase your profits.

Portfolio diversification

Investing in real estate can also help you diversify your investment portfolio. If you already have investments in the stock market or other forms of investments, adding real estate to your portfolio can help reduce your overall portfolio risk. Diversifying your investment portfolio is important to protect your money and increase your chances of long-term returns.

Stability and security

Real estate is a relatively stable and secure investment. Unlike investments in the stock market, real estate is not subject to market volatility and can provide a stable and reliable income over the long term. In addition, real estate can be a safe and tangible investment that you can see and touch.

Control and flexibility

Another advantage of investing in real estate is that you have more control and flexibility over your investment. You can choose the type of property you want to invest in, the location and the price, and you can also choose how to finance your investment. In addition, you can choose to hold the property for the long term and earn a steady income or sell it in the future for a profit.

Tax benefits

Investing in real estate can also have significant tax benefits. For example, you can deduct maintenance and repair costs from your taxes, which can significantly reduce the cost of the property. In addition, you may get additional tax benefits if you decide to sell the property in the future.

In short, there are many reasons to invest in real estate, from the long-term profit potential to the stability and security that real estate offers. Real estate investing can also help you diversify your investment portfolio, offer more control and flexibility over your investments and have significant tax benefits. If you are considering real estate investing, it is important to understand the pros and cons of this form of investment and to do your due diligence before making a decision. As we go through this book, we will further explore the different forms of real estate investment, how to choose the right property to invest in, how to finance your investment, and how to manage and maintain your properties.

I.IV Myths and Truths about Real Estate Investment (History)

Real estate investment is one of the oldest and most popular forms of investment in the world. However, like any form of investment, there are many myths and truths surrounding real estate investing. In this chapter, we will examine some of the most common myths and truths about real estate investing.

Myth 1: Real estate investment is only for the wealthy.

Truth: While it is true that real estate investing requires a significant amount of capital, it is not exclusive to wealthy individuals. There are many forms of real estate investment that do not require a large amount of capital, such as investing in real estate investment trusts, shared ownership and investing in commercial real estate.

Myth 2: Real estate investment always generates high returns

Truth: While real estate investing can be very profitable, it does not always generate large returns. Real estate investing is a long-term game and requires patience and strategy. And, like any investment, there is a risk of loss.

Myth 3: Real estate investment is passive and does not require work.

Truth: While it is true that real estate investing can generate passive income, it is not completely passive. Real estate investing requires work, effort and time, especially in the beginning. This includes searching for properties, conducting due diligence, negotiating prices, managing and maintaining properties.

Myth 4: Real estate investment is a safe form of investment.

Truth: While real estate investment may be more stable and secure than other forms of investment, it is not completely safe. The real estate market is susceptible to fluctuations and changes, and investors may experience losses in times of recession or economic downturn.

Myth 5: Only experts can invest in real estate

Truth: While real estate investing requires knowledge and experience, it is not exclusively for experts. Anyone can learn and improve their real estate investing skills with the right education and practice.

Myth 6: You Need to Own a Lot of Properties to Be Successful in Real Estate.

Truth: Success in real estate isn't about the quantity of properties you own, but rather the quality of your investments and how well they perform. Many successful investors have achieved great returns with just a handful of well-chosen properties.

Myth 7: Real Estate Investing is All About Timing the Market.

Truth: While market timing can influence outcomes, long-term success in real estate investing is more about location, property quality, and sound management. Consistent growth and income generation often come from good property fundamentals, not market speculation.

Myth 8: Investing in Real Estate Guarantees Immediate Cash Flow.

Truth: Real estate investments can take time to generate positive cash flow. Initial expenses, maintenance, and vacancies can affect earnings. Successful real estate investing often requires a strategic approach to ensure long-term cash flow.

Myth 9: Flipping Houses is Easy and Always Profitable.

Truth: Flipping houses can be lucrative, but it's not as simple as buying any property, making renovations, and selling for a profit. It requires market knowledge, renovation expertise, and timing. There's also a significant risk involved, as market conditions can change rapidly.

Myth 10: Real Estate Values Always Go Up.

Truth: While real estate has historically appreciated over time, there are periods where property values can stagnate or even decline. Real estate markets are cyclical, and values are influenced by economic conditions, demand, and other factors. Investors should be prepared for fluctuations and not assume constant appreciation.

In summary, in this chapter we have examined some of the most common myths and truths about real estate investing. It is important to understand these truths and myths in order to make informed decisions when investing in real estate. As you continue reading this book, we will further explore the different forms of real estate investing and how to make informed decisions to maximise your returns.

II. Financial planning for real estate investment

II.I SETTING FINANCIAL TARGETS

Real estate investing can be a valuable tool for achieving your long-term financial goals. However, to achieve success in real estate investing, it is essential to set clear and realistic financial goals.

Before investing in real estate, it is important to determine your financial goals. Are you looking to generate long-term passive income? Are you looking to build capital for future investment? Or are you looking for a way to diversify your investment portfolio? By establishing your financial goals, you will be able to identify which type of real estate investment is right for you.

Once you have established your financial goals, it is important to develop a detailed financial plan to achieve them. This includes determining how much capital you are willing to invest, how much time you are willing to invest, and what level of risk you are willing to take.

It is essential to carefully evaluate your personal finances to determine how much capital you are willing to invest. It is important to remember that investing in real estate requires a significant amount of upfront capital, and that cash flow will also be required to maintain the property. In addition, you should consider the costs associated with the investment, such as taxes, insurance and maintenance.

Once you have established your investment capital, it is important to determine how long you are willing to invest. Real estate investment is often a long-term investment, and can take several years to generate a significant return. You should consider how long you are willing to wait before you see a return on your investment.

It is also important to consider the level of risk you are willing to take in real estate investing. Real estate investing may be a more stable and secure investment compared to other forms of investment, but there are still risks associated with investing. You should consider what your risk tolerance is and select a real estate investment that fits it.

By setting financial goals and developing a detailed financial plan, you will be in a better position to achieve real estate investment success. In the next chapter, we will explore how to identify and evaluate real estate investment opportunities to select the right investment for your financial goals.

II.II Budget and savings

If you want to be a successful real estate investor, it is essential that you have a good handle on your personal finances. This includes learning how to budget and save effectively. In this chapter, we will discuss how to create a budget and how to save money for your real estate investments.

To begin with, it is important to understand that a budget is nothing more than planning your income and expenses. The purpose of creating a budget is to get a clear picture of your financial situation and how you can adjust your spending to meet your investment goals.

The first step in creating a budget is to determine your monthly income, either through your salary, business or investments. Next, identify your monthly expenses, such as utility bills, loan repayments, food and transportation. Once you have a clear idea of your income and expenses, you can create a list of priorities and adjust your spending to have more money available for saving and investing.

Another key aspect of successful real estate investment is learning to save effectively. Saving doesn't mean depriving yourself of everything, but rather prioritising your spending and finding ways to cut costs. This can include anything from cutting back on entertainment expenses to buying discounted items or using discount coupons.

An effective savings strategy is to set specific goals, for example, to save a specific percentage of your income each month. In addition, it is important to consider the time frame in which you want to reach your investment goals and adjust your spending accordingly.

It is important to note that the ability to save and budget is not something you learn overnight. It takes practice and patience, but once you have developed an effective savings habit, you will be able to apply this concept to your real estate investments and achieve your long-term financial goals.

II.III Assessment of borrowing capacity

In the world of real estate investment, debt capacity is a crucial factor that can determine whether or not you can obtain financing for your investment projects. It is important to have a clear understanding of your debt capacity before you start looking for investment properties.

Your borrowing capacity refers to the amount of money you can borrow to purchase a property, based on your ability to repay the loans. In other words, it is the maximum amount of debt you can take on without compromising your ability to repay.

To determine your borrowing capacity, lenders will assess your credit history, income and expenses. It is important to have a good credit history and maintain a low level of debt to improve your borrowing capacity. In addition, it is important to make sure you have a stable and sufficient income to pay your expenses and loan debt.

Once you have a clear understanding of your debt capacity, you can start looking for properties that fit your budget. It is important to keep in mind that you should not spend more than you can afford, even if you think the property is a great investment. Making sure you can afford your loan and expenses is essential to the long-term success of your investment.

II.IV Selection of the type of real estate investment

Once you have defined your financia goals and know how much you car invest, it is important to choose the type of real estate investment that is right for you. There are severa options available, and each has its own advantages and disadvantages.

Rental properties: Rental properties are a popular option for investors seeking regular income. These properties can be flats, houses or commercial buildings. The goal is to find tenants who will pay a monthly rent that will cover expenses and generate additional income. This option can also allow you to build long-term equity as the property increases in value.

Flipping: Investing in property to "flip" it involves buying a property, renovating it and selling it quickly at a higher price. This option is more suitable for more experienced investors, as it involves a higher risk and a larger initial investment.

Real estate crowdfunding investment: This option has become popular in recent years, especially for those seeking a more passive form of real estate investment. Instead of buying a physical property, investors can contribute to a fund that invests in multiple properties and receive a proportionate share of the proceeds.

Buy and hold: This option is similar to rental properties, but with a longer-term focus. Rather than seeking tenants for regular income, investors seek to acquire properties that will grow in value over the long term and be held for a longer period of time.

III. Property search and analysis

III.I Identification of investment opportunities

Once you have established your financial goals and understand the type of real estate investment that best suits your needs, it's time to start your property search.

The first consideration in the property search is location. The saying "location, location, location" still holds true in the real estate world, as location can have a major impact on the value and profitability of a property. Areas close to urban centres and areas of high demand are often the most attractive to property investors. Be sure to research the area carefully, including average property prices and market trends.

Once you have identified a suitable location, it is important to analyse specific properties. Start by establishing a budget and consider the purchase price, renovation costs and any other expenses associated with the property. It is also important to assess the rental potential and potential return on investment.

To find properties, there are several options available. You can search online, consult estate agents or attend property auctions. Each option has its pros and cons, so it is important to research and carefully consider each before making a decision.

Once you have found a property that interests you, it is important to conduct a thorough inspection. Be sure to examine the property inside and out, assess any damage or need for repair, and consider any structural or engineering problems. You should also check the property documents and verify that everything is in order.

III.II Analysis of the real estate market

Successful real estate investment relies heavily on the ability to analyse the market and identify current and future trends. A healthy real estate market is a critical factor for success in real estate investment.

In this chapter, we will look at the different factors that affect the real estate market and how they can impact your real estate investments. In addition, we will discuss how you can use market information to identify investment opportunities and make informed decisions about buying and selling real estate.

Factors affecting the real estate market:

Economic cycles: The real estate market is influenced by the economy in general. When the economy is booming, demand for housing and commercial property is usually high. However, in times of recession, demand decreases and prices may fall.

Demographic trends: Population growth and internal migration can have a significant impact on the real estate market. Cities experiencing population growth may have a higher demand for housing and commercial property, which increases prices.

Government policy: Government policies, such as changes in interest rates and tax incentives, can influence the real estate market.

Supply and demand: Supply and demand for real estate is a key factor influencing prices. When there is high demand and low supply, prices tend to rise.

How to analyse the real estate market:

Study market trends in the area in which you are interested in investing.

Compare prices of similar properties on the market.

Analyses the potential return on investment and return on investment.

It considers external factors that may influence the market, such as the economy and demographic trends.

In summary, to be successful in real estate investing, it is important to understand the factors affecting the market and to know how to analyse current and future trends. When investing in real estate, you need to be aware of changes in the economy, demographic trends and government policies. By analysing the real estate market and trends, you will be able to identify investment opportunities and make informed decisions about buying and selling real estate.

III.III Analysis of the return on investment

Once you have identified a real estate property that you consider a good investment opportunity, it is important to carry out a detailed analysis of the potential return. In this chapter, we will show you how to calculate the return on your investment and how to interpret the results.

There are several indicators that can be used to analyse the profitability of a real estate investment, including ROI (return on investment), cash on cash return, and cap rate. Let us look at each of these in more detail:

ROI: ROI is a measure of the return on an investment relative to the cost of the investment. To calculate ROI, divide the annual net income (total revenues minus total expenses) by the total cost of the investment (purchase price + closing costs + repair and improvement costs). Then multiply the result by 100 to express the ROI as a percentage. For example, if a property costs $100,000 and generates an annual net income of $10,000, the ROI would be 10%.

Cash on cash return: Cash on cash return is a measure of the return on an investment in relation to the capital invested. To calculate cash on cash return, divide the annual net income by the invested capital (i.e., the money you have invested in the property, excluding loans). For example, if a property costs $100,000 and you have invested $20,000 in cash, and it generates a net annual income of $10,000, the cash on cash return would be 50%.

Cap rate: The cap rate is a measure of the return earned on an investment relative to the market value of the property. To calculate the cap rate, divide the annual net income by the market value of the property. For example, if a property generates an annual net income of $10,000 and has a market value of $100,000, the cap rate would be 10%.

Another important indicator is the discounted cash flow (DCF), which takes into account future cash flows and discounts them to present value to determine the present value of the property. DCF is particularly useful for assessing the long-term profitability of a property.

It is also important to consider the cap rate, which is calculated by dividing the net operating income (NOI) of a property by its market value. The cap rate is often used to compare the profitability of different properties and real estate markets.

It is important to remember that these indicators should not be used in isolation, but in conjunction with other factors such as risk, inflation, potential for property value appreciation, among others. For example, a property that has a high ROI but is located in a high crime or economically declining area may be a risky investment.

To perform a detailed analysis of the profitability of an investment, it is necessary to consider several factors such as purchase price, closing costs, repair and improvement costs, rental income, operating expenses, taxes, insurance and financing costs. For example, if you plan to finance the investment, you should consider borrowing costs such as interest and fees.

It is important to do a market check to get an idea of market prices in the area where the property is located. You should also consider trends in the property market, as they may affect the value of the property in the future.

III.IV Assessment of ownership and location

In this chapter, we will discuss how to identify and evaluate real estate investment opportunities in order to select the right investment for your financial objectives.

The first thing to do is to research the property market. You should consider the location, the type of property and the general condition of the property. Location is an important factor to consider as it can affect the demand and value of the property. It is important to research the area and determine if there are any trends of growth or decline in demand.

You should also consider the type of property you wish to invest in. Investment options include flats, houses, commercial premises, land and industrial properties. Each type of property has its own advantages and disadvantages, and it is important to carefully evaluate each option before making a decision.

The overall condition of the property is another important factor to consider. If the property is in poor condition, it may require a significant amount of time and money to repair. On the other hand, if the property is in good condition, it may be easier to rent or sell.

Once you have researched the property market and selected the right type of property, it is important to determine the value of the property. There are several ways to determine the value of a property, such as comparing recent sales of similar properties in the same area or analysing the potential profitability of the property.

You should also consider the income potential of the property. If you plan to rent the property, you should consider the rent you can charge. If you plan to sell the property, you should consider the potential resale value.

In addition, it is important to consider the costs associated with ownership, such as taxes, insurance, maintenance and repairs. These costs should be taken into account when determining the potential return on investment.

In summary, in this chapter we have explored how to identify and evaluate real estate investment opportunities to select the right investment for your financial objectives. By researching the real estate market, selecting the right type of property, determining the value of the property, and considering the associated costs, you will be in a better position to make an informed decision about the right real estate investment for you. In the next chapter, we will discuss how to finance your real estate investment.

IV. Financing and property acquisition

IV.I Sources of funding

Sources of funding for real estate investment are crucial for investors looking to acquire property. Some of the most common options include mortgages, limited partnerships and real estate crowdfunding. Mortgages are a popular option that allow the investor to acquire a property in exchange for an interest-bearing loan for a set term. Limited partnerships, on the other hand, are a way of structuring joint ownership of a property, especially for large-scale properties. Real estate crowdfunding is a relatively new option that allows investors to contribute small amounts of money to finance a particular real estate project.

It is important to note that the investor must carefully evaluate the costs associated with the acquisition of the property and assess the risk and expected return on the investment. For example, if an investor wants to purchase a $500,000 property and opts for a 30-year 4% interest mortgage, he would have to pay $343,585 in interest over the entire term of the loan. On the other hand, if the investor enters into a limited partnership with two other investors and each contributes $166,666 towards the acquisition of the property, they would have to consider management agreements and maintenance costs, but could earn an attractive return if the property is profitable.

Mortgages: This is a popular option for acquiring property, especially for investors who do not have the ability to pay cash. In general, mortgages are offered by banks and financial institutions, and allow the investor to acquire a property in exchange for a loan, to be repaid with interest over a certain period of time.

The most common option for financing the acquisition of a real estate property is through a mortgage loan. This type of financing is offered by banks and other financial institutions and allows the investor to obtain the necessary capital to acquire the property in exchange for a commitment to pay within a certain period of time.

One of the main characteristics of mortgage loans is that they are backed by the property itself, which means that in case of default, the lender can take possession of the property to recover its investment. For this reason, financial institutions usually request an appraisal of the property before granting the loan, in order to assess the real value of the property and ensure that the investment is secure.

Another important feature of mortgage loans is the repayment term, which can vary according to the type of loan and the financial institution. In general, the terms range from 10 to 30 years, and the monthly payments include both the capital loaned and the interest generated by the loan.

In addition, it is common for mortgage loans to include a fixed or variable interest rate, which can influence the total amount of monthly payments and the total cost of the loan. Fixed interest rates ensure that the monthly payment will remain constant throughout the term of the loan, while variable rates can fluctuate according to market conditions.

It is important for the investor to carefully evaluate the available mortgage loan options before making a decision, as interest rates, terms and other factors may vary considerably among financial institutions. In addition, it is recommended that the investor has a good credit history and sufficient financial capacity to meet the loan payments on time.

Limited partnerships: also known as LLCs, are a way of structuring joint ownership of a property, where investors can contribute a portion of the capital needed to acquire the property. This option is common for large-scale properties, such as commercial buildings or housing complexes.

The option of financing through limited partnerships, also known as LLCs, is a popular alternative for investors interested in acquiring large-scale real estate. In this type of investment structure, the members of the LLC contribute a certain amount of capital to the acquisition of the property and share in the liability and profits of the investment.

The following are some of the most relevant characteristics of limited companies:

Limited liability: One of the main advantages of limited companies is that members have limited liability, meaning that their liability is limited to the amount of capital they have invested. This helps protect investors' personal assets in case of legal or financial problems.

Flexibility in partnership structure: LLCs allow for great flexibility in the partnership structure and in the arrangements for distribution of profits and liabilities among the members. This can be especially beneficial in situations where members have different financial or investment needs.

Taxation: Limited partnerships are flexible tax entities and can be treated as pass-through, meaning that income and losses are passed through to members and reported on their personal tax returns. This can be beneficial in reducing the tax burden on investors.

Registration and maintenance requirements: Limited partnerships must register in the state where they are incorporated and must comply with certain maintenance requirements, such as filing annual reports and keeping accurate records.

It is important to note that limited partnerships can be a complex option and require careful planning and legal and financial advice before implementation. It is also important to carefully assess the risk and expected return on investment, as well as the agreement on the distribution of profits and liabilities among the members.

In summary, limited partnerships are an attractive option for investors seeking to acquire large-scale real estate and share the responsibility and benefits of the investment. However, it is important to carefully assess the risks and benefits, as well as to obtain legal and financial advice prior to implementation.

Real estate crowdfunding is a relatively new option that allows investors to contribute small amounts of money to finance a particular real estate project. This option is accessible to a wide range of investors and can be an easy and cost-effective way to diversify an investment portfolio.

Real estate crowdfunding is a relatively new option that allows investors to contribute small amounts of money to finance a particular real estate project. This option is accessible to a wide range of investors and can be an easy and cost-effective way to diversify an investment portfolio.

Some key characteristics of real estate crowdfunding are described below:

Accessible to a wide range of investors: Unlike traditional real estate investment, which generally requires large amounts of capital, real estate crowdfunding allows investors to contribute small amounts of money to fund a project. This makes real estate investment accessible to a wide range of investors, including those with more limited budgets.

Portfolio diversification: By investing in real estate crowdfunding, investors have the opportunity to diversify their investment portfolio more easily. Instead of investing large sums of money in a single property, investors can contribute small amounts of money in several different real estate projects.

Transparency: Real estate crowdfunding projects are usually very transparent and provide a great deal of information about the project in which they are investing. This allows investors to make more informed decisions about their investment and to carefully assess the risk and expected return on investment.

Potential returns: While real estate crowdfunding may involve higher risk than other forms of real estate investment, it can also offer potentially higher returns. By diversifying investment across multiple projects, investors can increase their profit potential.

In summary, real estate crowdfunding can be an attractive option for investors looking to diversify their investment portfolio and access real estate investment opportunities on a limited budget. However, it is important for investors to carefully assess the risk and expected return of each project before investing their money.

It is important to note that regardless of the source of financing chosen, the investor must take into account the costs associated with acquiring the property and carefully assess the risk and expected return on investment. In general, investors should seek a financing mix that allows them to minimise risk while maximising the return on their investment.

IV.II Property acquisition process

Each of the key steps in the real estate acquisition process has important details that must be taken into account to ensure a successful and profitable investment.

First of all, property identification involves a thorough research of the local real estate market. The investor must define his or her investment criteria, such as location, size and specific property characteristics, and search for properties that meet these criteria. Once a potential property has been identified, a careful evaluation of the property must be carried out.

Property evaluation is a crucial step in the process of acquiring a real estate property. It involves conducting a detailed inspection of the property, reviewing the property records and evaluating its income and expense history. This evaluation will provide valuable information to determine the true value of the property and its investment potential.

Once the property has been appraised, the price should be negotiated with the seller. It is important to make an offer based on the valuation of the property and negotiate the terms of the transaction, such as payment term and mortgage terms.

If financing is required to acquire the property, the investor must obtain mortgage loan approval or seek other forms of financing, such as limited partnership investment or real estate crowdfunding. It is important to obtain the necessary financing for the acquisition of the property before proceeding with the closing of the transaction.

The closing of the transaction is the last step in the process of acquiring a real estate property. It involves preparing the necessary legal documents, signing the contracts and transferring the property to the buyer. It is important to carry out this step carefully and to ensure that all conditions agreed in the negotiation of the price and terms of the transaction have been met.

In conclusion, the real estate acquisition process is complex and requires a number of important steps. It is essential to carry out each of these steps carefully to ensure that the transaction is carried out efficiently and effectively, and to maximise the potential for investment and profitability.

IV.III Legal and fiscal aspects

Investing in real estate not only involves financial aspects, but also has important legal and tax implications that investors should carefully consider. In this chapter, we will discuss some of the key legal and tax issues related to real estate investment and the associated tax and fiscal advantages.

Legal aspects of real estate investment:

Before making any real estate investment, it is important to understand the laws and regulations governing real estate. This may include zoning laws, building regulations, and other legal aspects and regulations related to the property. In addition, it is important to be aware of any building permit and compliance requirements that may be necessary to carry out a successful real estate investment.

Tax aspects of real estate investment:

Investing in real estate also has significant tax implications. Some of the most common taxes and tax advantages associated with real estate investment are described below:

Property tax: is a tax levied on real estate property and is based on the value of the property. This tax is paid by the property owner and can be a significant expense for real estate investors.

Income tax: Income generated by investment in real estate may be subject to income tax. Income taxes may vary depending on the type of property and the structure of the property.

Tax advantages of real estate investment:

Despite the taxes associated with real estate investment, there are a number of tax advantages that investors can take advantage of. Some of these advantages include:

Expense deductions: Investors can deduct certain property-related expenses, such as mortgage interest and maintenance costs, which can significantly reduce the amount of tax they have to pay.

Property depreciation: Depreciation is an expense that allows investors to deduct the cost of property over time. This deduction can significantly reduce the amount of tax investors have to pay.

In conclusion, real estate investment is a popular choice for many investors due to its potential for profitability. However, it is important to consider the legal and tax aspects of the investment to ensure a successful and profitable investment. The tax and fiscal advantages described above are just some of the factors that should be considered when making a real estate investment.

V. Conclusions and recommendations

In conclusion, investing in real estate can be an excellent option for earning passive income and building long-term wealth. However, it is important to keep in mind certain tips for successful investing and avoid common mistakes that can negatively affect the return on your investment.

Tips for successful real estate investing include the importance of thorough market and property research, careful assessment of the costs and risks associated with the investment, and diversification of the investment portfolio.

On the other hand, it is essential to avoid common mistakes such as lack of planning and underestimation of costs, lack of market and property knowledge, and lack of patience for long-term returns.

In addition, it is important to consider the future prospects of the real estate market and real estate investment. As the world changes and evolves, real estate investment opportunities also change. Investors need to be aware of market trends and adapt to them in order to take advantage of opportunities.

In conclusion, real estate investing can be an excellent option for investors seeking to diversify their portfolios and earn passive income over the long term. By following tips for successful investing, avoiding common mistakes and keeping abreast of the future prospects of the real estate market, investors can achieve a successful and profitable investment in real estate.

www.ingramcontent.com/pod-product-compliance
Lightning Source LLC
Chambersburg PA
CBHW071028220526
45467CB00004B/1566